ALL THAT WE HAD W\

Copyright: Peter Glyr

ALL THAT WE HAD , W

by

Peter Glynn

" All that we had , we gave,

All that was ours to give;

Freely surrendered all

That you in peace might live.

In trench and field and many seas we lie

We who in dying shall not ever die,

If only you in honour of the slain

Shall surely see we did not die in vain."

The year is 1914. Large scale casualties to the British regular army mean that the Denbigh Territorials are thrown into the inferno of the Western Front.

This is a war of rain , mud , bullets , shells and blood.

The vicious fight against the forces of the Kaiser in the first year of the Great War would have a devastating effect on the families of Denbigh.

This is the story of the Denbigh Terriers – of ordinary men who served in exceptional times – a story of duty , courage and of the supreme sacrifice.

Introduction

In the industrial town of Bethune , Northern France , lies a cemetery. The uneven and multifarious graves of the townsfolk stretch as far as the eye can see ; and the cinder path that is trodden on a hot and dusty late summer's afternoon seems interminable.

All at once the eye of the visitor is drawn to row after row of pristine white headstones that mark the final resting place of hundreds upon hundreds of British and Dominion soldiers killed in the early years of the Great War.

In most instances the headstones are set close together , suggesting mass rather than individual burial. Some have no name inscribed and simply read ' A Soldier of the Great War ' or ' Known unto God.'

Whilst in their home towns these men are all but forgotten with the passage of time , the stillness of Bethune Cemetery is interrupted by the gentle humming of a lawn mower or the clicking of garden shears as the workmen employed by the Commonwealth Grave Commission continue to tend each individual plot as they have done for decades.

It is here that the grave of a Denbigh man can be found. Private Albert Edward Myddleton , 4th Battalion , Royal Welsh Fusiliers (Territorial Force) was one of countless thousands killed in the 'war to end all wars'. One would have hoped that Ted had not died in vain . Unfortunately the Great War decided very little , for within 21 years German tanks were rolling past the iron gates of this very cemetery on their way to Paris.

Three quarters of a million British officers and men had perished to preserve the freedom of Belgium and France from 1914 until 1918 , but all that remains of their sacrifice now are row upon row of these white headstones in similar cemeteries scattered around the world.

The First World War affected every family in Britain like no conflict before or since. Almost every family lost a close relative , some more than one. Denbigh was no exception and the town's sacrifice can be found in graveyards in every part of the conflict , starting on the Western Front from Ypres in the north , down through Arras and southwards to the chalky Somme battlefields ; out in Easter Europe , in Salonika and Bulgaria , into Turkish Gallipoli , and further south again into the deserts of Palestine , Mesopotamia and East Africa, On the high seas and at the bottom of the Atlantic Ocean. Beneath the azure of the Mediterranean Sea. Denbigh's war touched every part of the conflict.

The town's military service started with the Regulars who held up the German advance into Belgium and France long enough for the Allies to counter attack at the Battle of the Aisne. Now the war became static , with German and allied trenches stretching from the English Channel to Switzerland. One Denbigh man who fought to keep the Germans from this breakthrough was Private Cyril Rutter of the 1st. Battalion Cheshire Regiment. He was to spend the rest of his young life in a prison camp and died on the eve of peace.

The flower of Denbigh's youth would be all but plucked on the battlefields of the Somme between July 1st and November 18th 1916 , where some of our brightest stars winked out ; solicitor Reg Knowles , grocer's lad Thomas William Jones , draper Albert Edward Jones , just three of many from the town who fought and died in that hopeless cause.

Finally, in the mud and chaos of Passchendaele, when both counties gasped to almost their last breath in the search for victory, Denbigh was bleeding still. Tom Williams from Temple Bar Square, Owen Williams of Boderw and Hugh Edward Davies who worked in Denson's, laid down their precious future in the desperate bid for a breakthrough.

It was only a matter of time before one or the other of the combatants would collapse. And ultimately it was Germany, its resources and manpower bled white by the five year campaign that most thought would last but a few months, who ended the greatest conflict in earth's history on her knees, yet only to rise up in fury in 1939 to plunge the world into war once more.

1915 was the year of the Territorial. An accurate and full historical account of the Denbighites and others who fought as Terriers in this period of the war will probably never be written. Censorship and a lack of research when memories were fresh and first hand means that the full human story will never be comprehensively told.

Self censorship too plays its part, with most combatants reluctant to relive their experiences. The historical side of 1915 has been somewhat passed over with other more well known battles capturing the dominant share of Great War research.

This is an attempt to redress this in a small way. It is about ordinary men, Denbigh men who were expected to be soldiers in conditions that will never be experienced again. How they managed to cope with their duty on the Western Front, and how they came to terms with the memories of it during the rest of their lives after the war was ended will remain a mystery.

The Denbigh Terriers

The start of the war saw the British Infantry made up of Regiments consisting of either one or two Battalions, with a Reserve Battalion based at the 'Depot', the permanent home headquarters.

Added to this, in some cases, were Territorial Battalions formed in 1908 out of the old 'Volunteers' and whose purpose was for home service only.

Their function was to step into the breach and guard the country during war time when the regular Battalions were fighting overseas. Most wars fought by the British were against restless natives of the Empire and though give a bloody nose in South Africa, China and several of the Indian uprisings, the regulars eventually sorted things out to the satisfaction of the politicians and general public at home.

The outbreak of war in August 1914 saw many of the regular Battalions of the British Army in various garrisons around the expansive Empire.: Malta, India, Jamaica, South Africa and nearer to home in Ireland. And whilst the ' Old Contemptibles' were holding back the Germans in the early weeks, it was decided to man these foreign garrisons with Territorial Battalions to protect British interests and thereby release more regular Battalions for front line service.

But casualty returns in Flanders were so heavy that a decision was made to send some Territorial units to the front as soon as practicable, a decision which was unpopular in many quarters of the War Department.

It was really a matter of luck as to where each of the Territorial Battalions were sent, but some were deemed more ready for war than others and these were selected to bolster the weakened army now taking a hammering in Flanders.

The 4th (Territorial) Battalion, Royal Welsh Fusiliers were one of the very first of its kind to be sent over to France. They were part of the North Wales Territorial Infantry Brigade and in August on declaration of war were immediately moved to Conway and at the end of the month to Northampton. On 6th November they landed in Le Havre and on the 1st December were transferred to the 3rd Brigade of General Haig's 1st Army Division.

Their destination was the Western Front with certain responsibilities to General Staff Headquarters. These were to set up lines of communication between GHQ and the front line troops, but in effect it meant that they were expected to do anything required of them, such as escorting prisoners, transporting ammunition, securing front line gains or acting as support or reserve infantry.

An Army Division was commanded by a Major General and was made up of Infantry, Artillery and Engineers. The Royal Field Artillery worked side by side with the Infantry, shelling or bombarding the enemy, or providing a barrage – a French term whereby heavy fire is brought down upon a certain section of land. The Royal Engineers were split into Field Companies and Signals Companies. During the first months of the war it was they who blew the bridges over the rivers to hold up the German advance, built pontoons and dug the first trenches occupied by the Infantry, always under the severest of enemy fire.

Any repair to the barbed wire or trench was also undertaken by the RE. After January 1915, the Infantry were expected to make good their own repairs as necessary.

A Division consisted of three Brigades, usually of the same type, i.e. Regular, Territorial or New Army (post 1916). A Brigade came under the command of a Brigadier General, and consisted of four Battalions. Each Battalion was commanded by a Lieutenant Colonel and was made up of 35 officers and one thousand other ranks, this being deemed 'full strength'.

By September 1915, when the General Staff realised that trench warfare was continuing to dominate the war on the Western Front, 'Pioneer' Battalions were introduced to each Division. After September 1915, the 4th Battalion RWF became a pioneer Battalion and were allocated to the 47th (London) Division.

The rankers in Pioneer Battalions were generally made up of working class men used to physical work down the mines or on the roads or in the building industry. With hindsight, belonging to a 'Pioneer' Battalion had its advantages. They avoided such slaughters as experienced by men at Festubert, the Somme and at Passchendaele, where so many lives were lost for a few yards. However there remained great dangers, as Pioneer parties were subject to intense German shelling and counter attacks whilst digging to secure new gains in the front line.

The trickle of casualties, both dead and wounded, mostly accounts for the horrifying overall figure of three quarters of a million British lives lost.

So between their arrival in France in November 1914 and until the Battle of Festubert in May 1915, the Denbigh Terriers were designated to all intents and purposes, front line infantry.

The war had become immobile and the Germans held the high ground, be it a hillock or a simply rise in the pastures. The baton had now been passed to the Territorial Battalions and it is they that were to bear the brunt until reinforcements in Kitchener's recruitment campaign could arrive.

The 4th RWF, Denbighshire Battalion was made up of Companies recruited from specific areas of the county. This allowed friend, colleague and family member to join up together, work together, feel encouraged to join the colours, and help with feelings of comradeship, civic pride, discipline, morale and other positives in belonging to a close military unit from within one's own town.

The benefits of belonging to a Territorial unit – at least in peace time – ranged from the prestige (and uniform to go with it) to a holiday in summer camp once a year. The ranks were thoroughly trained, the officers traditionally ex-Regular and the N.C.O.s of a character to match any in the British Army.

But there were suspicions in the War Office that its close knitted-ness would be a problem on the field of battle and that discipline may be somewhat lax.

'A' and 'B' Companies were Wrexham men, 'C' was filled with Ruabonites. 'D' Company was the good old Denbigh and Ruthin Company. The remainder down to the letter 'H' came from the Wrexham AREA - Coedpoeth, Gwersyllt, Rhos, Chirk and Llangollen.

Each Company came under the responsibility of a Captain and usually contained five other officers, Lieutenants or 2nd Lieutenants. Add to this 250 other ranks. This in turn was split into Platoons, with 60 men under the leadership of a 2nd Lieutenant. Broken down further, a Sergeant or Corporal would take charge of Sections consisting of 14 men.

On 4th August, the Denbighshire Territorials – The 'Terriers' – were almost up to full strength at their summer camp at Devil's Bridge in Aberystwyth. 29 officers, and 993 men had arrived at their annual training camp with three other Territorial Battalions of the North Wales Infantry Brigade, namely the 5th (Flintshire), 6th (Caernarfonshire and Anglesey), and 7th (Meirioneth and Montgomery).

The 4th were the most up-to-strength Battalion in the camp and it was considered that the officers were well trained and the men, mainly colliers from the mines of Wrexham, in perfect physical condition for war. That was what the newspapers reported. But maybe this was based on campaigns fought in the past, against ill equipped natives in far flung corners of the Empire. What these men were about to sign up for was something nobody had imagined.

In the meantime, it was with a sense of eagerness and with a swagger that the camp broke up and returned home to prepare for war.

From Summer Camp to the Trenches

Denbigh has a military background as old as the Castle itself, and the male population were eager to enlist, and they had two distinct Territorial battalions to volunteer to join, namely the Denbigh Hussars Imperial Yeomanry (DHIY) and the 4th (Denbighshire) Battalion R.W.F. (T.F.).

Like all towns and cities across Britain, the war began to dominate all aspects of life and created a carnival like atmosphere within the town. Lots of patriotic bunting and flags began to appear. Businesses were eager to be seen helping the preparation for war and most people believed it was right and proper to tackle German imperialism and culture.

The sounds of military bugles were heard throughout Denbigh and the arrival of the DHIY added to the mood, adding spectacle and colour. 'B' Squadron of the Yeomanry represented the towns of Rhyl, Abergele, Denbigh and Ruthin. Their depot was in Park Street. The troopers were billeted in lodgings, hotels and public houses across town and their horses were stabled in Back Row, Hawk and Buckle, The Talbot and the Railway Hotel. Squadron Sergeant Carey, well known in Denbigh, was in charge of the troopers and was busy with paperwork as the men started to sign in. He was also responsible for organising the training of troopers and horses which always attracted a crowd. Meantime, sentries were posted in the depot and at the stables, adding to the martial climate of the time.

Another busy institution was the Post Office. It was kept open day and night with 200 to 300 telegrams passing back and forth. Local Girl Guides were used to deliver the masses of correspondence now flooding the town.

The Terriers now gathered in full strength, but an announcement was made calling upon retired members of the 4th to re-enlist as many in the current Battalion were too young for active service. Reporting as full strength, the D Company paraded in front of the Drill Hall and marched off in military order, led by a goat to a rousing send off by the excited locals. Captain W.C.B William and Lieutenant Gronwy Griffith were in command, accompanied by Sergeant Instructor Carless, Colour-Sergeant Tommy Roberts and Sergeants John O.Thomas , John Henry Emmanuel and Robert Williams. They took the 420pm train to Plas Power Camp in Bersham, their Batallion depot.

Reservists were now asked to assemble at the Drill Hall and the following re-enlisted with an bounty of £10 : Jeremiah Davies, of 17 Factory Place, David Jones, Reg Lewis, Robert William Ellis, Joseph Atkinson, John Foulkes, John Davies, Thomas Hugh Myddleton, Edward Jones, Ferguson Jones, John W. Jones, John Parry, Ellis Jones, William Roberts, Robert Jones and Edward Jones, Philip Tallents (Tremeirchion). Subsequently these men joined their Battalion in Conwy.

Officer commanding the 4th RWF was Lieutenant Colonel Frederick France Hayhurst of Bostock Hall, Middlewich. Major A.E. Johnson (a veteran of the Boer War with the RWF) was his second in command. Adjutant (a position quite similar to secretary) was Captain John Randle Minshull-Ford. The Battalion Quartermaster was Captain Thomas Manfield. Manfield was quite a character, known for his stories, some quite racy. He was commissioned Quartermaster with an honorary rank of Lieutenant in 1912, direct from his service as a Colour-Sergeant and Acting Sergeant-Major in the 4th RWF. He was granted a rank of QM and Major on his retirement from the Regiment in July 1927. He was awarded an MBE (Military Division) in 1925.

The Officers of 'D' Company were Lieutenant W.C.B. Williams of Llewesog Hall, Lieutenant Peter Foulkes-Roberts of Denbigh, 2nd Lieutenant Gronwy Robert Griffith, Garn, Henllan.

The strength of D Company assembling at Wrexham was 73 other ranks. More were arriving each day.

A crowd gathered to see off the Denbighshire Yeomanry who parading before making their way to Eccleston Camp, off Rake Lane on the Eaton Estate, south of Chester. It was a colourful sight with some troopers wearing their scarlet uniforms and blue pillbox head-wear. Here in Eccleston, they were joined by the remainder of the Welsh Border Mounted Brigade. On 3rd September it must have been a sight when the whole camp rode out towards Chester, and entered the city centre to load 2000 men and 1500 horses onto 13 trains bound for Norwich from Northgate Station. Chester Cattle Market was used to feed and water the horses.

The 4th RWF were now ordered to move from Wrexham to Conway to join with other Territorials gathering under canvas there. Their camp was on Conway Marsh. Lt. Peter Foulkes-Roberts had been travelling on his motor cycle every day between Denbigh and Wrexham, but he joined the transfer by railway, the train stopping in Denbigh for 15 minutes at 1130am on 22nd August to pick up more Terriers.

On Conway Marsh it was three to a tent. Peter Foulkes-Roberts helped organise basic training, drilling, route marches and guard duty. The 4th RWF were ordered to guard the tubular bridge at Conway and other parts of the railway line from German sabotage. There was an element of paranoia sweeping the country and the spotlight of distrust had settled on all German nationals living the Britain. A notice was pinned to the wall of Denbigh Police Station It read

" Alien registration. Order in Council Registration. Notice is hereby given that Aliens of German nationality are required to register themselves forthwith. They should apply immediately to the nearest Police Station for instructions. By order of the Secretary of state for the Home Department. Penalty, a fine of £100 or imprisonment for 6 months."

The attention of a constable was drawn to a crowd gathering in Back Row. A stranger had appeared in town, speaking a funny accent and unable to speak the Welsh language. He was wearing unusual garments and it became increasingly clear in some minds that here was a German spy, no doubt looking to cause awful damage to the town of Denbigh and its residents. On investigation, the police constable discovered that the stranger was not a German saboteur at all. He sent this 'Gentleman of the Road' on his way, presumable back to Chester from whence he had come.

Back in Conway, preparations were being made to transfer the Denbighshire Terriers to Northampton. On 31st August at 9am, the Battalion paraded in full army uniform in the Market Square of Northampton. As the rest of Britain's young men rushed to the recruiting stations (Lieutenant King was in charge of the Denbigh Recruiting Station at 2 Post Office

Lane), and those now enlisting began to parade in civilian clothing, The Territorials of Denbigh were already looking like the real thing.

Their Officers were drawn from the Regular Army, a tradition which continued until most had been wiped out by mid 1915, and it was noticed in parade that some of the Officers wore the 'flash' of black ribbons at the back of their caps, which hung down over their collars. Some on-lookers thought it was a relic of when the Royal Welsh wore pigtails, whilst others argued that the flash represented the Prince of Wales feathers.

The weather was very fine and heavy khaki was replaced in most cases with a new linen uniform. Lieutenant Peter Foulkes Roberts was struck down with tomach pains and did not have the opportunity to try his new issue. The Medical Officer diagnosed appendicitis and the Adjutant (Mr. Minshull-Ford) wrote to Peter's father, a well known solicitor in the town, telling him of his son's imminent surgical operation. Members of the family made their way to Northampton, and stayed at the Ram Hotel. The operation was carried out by surgeon Dr. Milligan. Peter was now out of the war until June 1915. He would yet see action aplenty.

Gradually the total Territorials gathering in Northampton grew to 16,000 which was a welcome sight to some home owners, as the army paid 9d a day for housing a ranker and 3s for an officer.

However there were not many more houses than visitors so, added to the 7000 horses brought into Northampton, most were accommodated on the racecourse which also acted as a parade ground.

'D' Company, being early arrivals, were housed in the town, though were split in their billets. One half were quartered in a room in the Liberal Club, the other half in a Working Man's Club *" with a blanket for a bed."*

The men were up at 5 o'clock each morning, breakfast followed work at 7 o'clock. There was some P.E. Which was followed by route marches and training. Dinner was taken in the fields, usually in front of an audience of civilians who would watch from a distance and later on, shower the men with gifts of food and flowers. Parades took place at 5 o'clock each evening, and tea was taken at 6 o'clock. Concerts each evening kept the men occupied and bed time was 9.30 p.m. Occasionally there were night marches. The only complaints from the men was of sore feet. 70 pairs of socks were sent down courtesy of the Voluntary Aid Detachment Working Committee in Denbigh under Mrs. Lilian Gregson-Ellis, Mrs. Mildred Hughes and Mrs. Catherine Swayne.

A little black kitten, named Tango, could usually be found asleep in someone's cap in the billet. As for the locals :*" The people are kind and we always get cheers as all are fond of the Welsh. They like to hear Welsh hymns."*

Nobody knew what was to become of them. One Terrier wrote home that they were going overseas to India on garrison duty. Over 800men and N.C.O.s of the 4th RWF had volunteered for overseas service, something not required of them as Territorial soldiers. History shows over 90% of Territorials throughout Britain did indeed sign up for service abroad.

Another 200 recruits were needed to bring the Regiment up to full strength. Some were on their way down from Denbighshire. A training base for these was set up in Bedford, Cambridge (Abbey Road) and Norwich, which was shared with the Denbighshire Yeomanry.

By 5th November the orders were to depart Northampton for France. The 4th RWF had been selected to become part of the 3rd Brigade in the 1st Army Division. They were to make ready for the Western Front.

A rousing send off was given them by the good folk of Northampton, though at times it settled into farce as a new supply of fresh clothing, socks, boots, shirts etc. were thrown at the men by officers as they marched their way to the railway station.

Some crying and sounds of anguish were heard from relatives and friends gathered on the platforms, but finally the men of 'A', 'B', 'C' and 'D' Companies, under the severe eye of senior NCO Sergeant Palmer, departed on railway carriages for Southampton at 10am, with much waving of handkerchiefs and Union flags. The other Companies followed on the 1pm train.

That night at half past eleven, the 4th clambered aboard the troopship 'Architect' which was docked in the port of Southampton, their destination Le Havre, France, one of the main ports that the allies used during the war. There proved to be a massive hold up on arrival due to the number of ships attempting to disembark their men and cargo.

The battalion were forced to endure a seven hour delay on board the 'Architect'.

Once off the ship, the Battalion was organised into ranks and immediately began a three mile march to a rest camp in Bleville.

The fog made marching difficult and with no field kitchens there were no stops for drinks. Each man had his own billy can which could be warmed but too too long to generate any heat for a satisfying drink of tea.

The Terriers rested for one day in Bleville Camp before marching to the local railway station and loaded on cattle trucks, heading north east to St. Omer. The journey was punctuated by frequent stops for no evident reason, and the men reported that it was the most tedious of journeys. Then on arrival at St. Omer they were housed for a few hours in a French cavalry barracks to rest and eat, before another march took the weary men to Heuringhem five miles to the south.

The sound of the guns of war was now within earshot. They were thirty miles from the front line and were to remain in Heuringhem for the next month. Always in the background, the guns could be heard.

The training now became more intense. Route marches were organised each day, often for six or seven miles. Bayonet and musket training were followed by attacking through quagmires. The wet weather added to the toil of training. As for the locals, they seemed unaware that there was a war going on and went about their business as usual, though selling items to souvenir hunting Tommies became a new cottage industry.

The arrival in France meant a reorganisation of the Battalion to conform with the 1914 directive from the War Office. This order reduced the number of Companies from eight to four. The majority of the Denbigh boys remained in 'D' Company, but some were now placed in other Companies. Alf Boyes (Henllan Street) went to 'C' Company. Will Owen Roberts to 'B' Company.

The condition of the footwear was giving concern. This was ironic as the centre of the shoe industry, Northampton, was the place they had been stationed prior to arriving at the war. Soles were beginning to peel away from the boots (some soles were sent home in parcels as souvenirs.) A Shoe-smith Sergeant was summoned and he worked for four weeks repairing the damage sustained in the heavy training schedules.

Back in Denbigh, mail was coming through. But there was no news as to where exactly the Terriers had been sent. Postcards and letters were heavily censored as to any detail of their whereabouts, arriving without postmarks or address, stating only " With The Expeditionary Force."

Local newspapers were beginning to grumble as they were becoming desperate for news of their new heroes. " *It would do no harm*", read one editorial, " *to let families know whether they be in India, Egypt or France.*"

But to be fair to the B.E.F. Information did begin to trickle through to the families and the press started printing quite freely from letters received.

By the end of November 'D' Company were settling in well into life overseas. There were some promotions in the ranks for some : William David Davies to Sergeant, and in 'C' Company, Alfred Boyes to Corporal., Lincoln Miller to Corporal and Wallace Roberts (The Crown Livery Stables) to Sergeant. David Davies (Lamplighter) had been promoted to Corporal.

Gifts of tobacco and cigarettes found their way to the boys now nearing the end of their training, this usually within three to five days of being posted from Denbigh. These gifts helped keep the spirits of the men high.

By the start of December, preparations were made to move further up towards the front line. The trenches were a march away. Captain Frederick Clough was struck down with ill health and rheumatism.

Sergeant Instructor Carless : " *We are not far from it, we are, according to the routine, next for the trenches. The 1st RWF have suffered heavily, more I cannot say. I am sorry to say that Captain Clough is not with us and I am sure the boys think the same. No-one is in particular bad health here.*"

Captain Clough is Frederick Burton Clough, owner of Clough & Co., Auctioneers. He was very well known in town, not only as Captain of the Denbigh contingent of Volunteers, but also as an Alderman of the Town Council and as Chairman of Denbigh Town Football Club. And he was a vice-President of the North Wales Coast FA. Many Denbigh town footballers were serving, Warren Lewis, Arthur Lewis, Thomas Albert Davies and Jack Thomas were with the 4th RWF.

Captain Clough had been retained at home for training and recruitment, due to his age, but during a public meeting had spoken up for increasing the age of those being allowed overseas to 40 years. Mr. Clough himself was 40 years old. His wish was granted and he was overseas with his fellow Terriers until being now invalided home. He was anxious to be back in France as soon as possible.

Despite Sergeant Carless's assurances, bad health was a concern. The wet and cold weather, lack of warm clothing and worn out boots were responsible for cold and in some cases pneumonia, resulting in casualties before a shot had been fired their way.

The weather was to prove very miserable throughout the next three months. This was one of the great trials of the soldiers. Weather and bad food.

Pte. Robert Jones was reported dead. He was seventeen years old. He was suffering from severe pneumonia. His family in Wesley Place received a letter from the War Office reporting his death in hospital. He re-emerged in January in a hospital in Leeds. This after a remembrance service attended by all his family and friends in town.

Sergeant John Owen Thomas and his son Jackie Thomas were together in France. John, the father, a stalwart of 'D' Company, was struck down with severe illness and was invalided home. He would not return to France.

Major Algernon Johnson suffered frostbite and rheumatism and he returned to Blighty to concentrate his efforts on recruiting and training.

Replacements were sought and were forthcoming. Twenty year old Thomas Godfrey Edwards left his job in Crewe to join the Battalion. He was the son of Volunteer Sergeant T. Godfrey Edwards, a painter and decorator from Love Lane. Volunteer Sergt. Edwards was busy in the war effort in Denbigh, organising the Voluntary Training Corps. Reservist Wallace Roberts of Park Street, a Corporal, was immediately promoted to Sergeant on joining the Terriers currently in Heuringhem.

The Terriers were now ordered to quit Heuringhem and march to a camp in Bailleul, a small town two miles from the border with Belgium, which was used for billets, headquarters and medical united. There was a Royal Flying Corps aerodrome just outside town.

The first ravages of war were becoming evident, firstly the sight of hundreds of wounded Tommies on the way to hospital ships in Le Havre. One of the wounded called out to the Denbigh men *"Are we downhearted?" "NO!"* came the reply. *" Well, you bloody well soon will be"* was the punchline delivered by one battered Tommy.

Next a pitiful stream of Belgian refugees came into Bailleul, carrying with them what possessions they could from their homes and farms. The war was now getting closer.

Once settled, the men were addressed by Divisional Commander, Major-General David Henderson and then by Brigade Commander, Brigadier Richard Butler (Later Sir Richard Harte Keatinge Butler.). This meant something but they weren't sure what.

Colonel France Hayhurst now took the opportunity to inspect his Battalion and found twenty lads underage. The records of the RWF describe what happened :

"Colonel France-Hayhurst ordered a parade of those who were 17 years of age or younger. About twenty paraded and were individually asked by the CO: "Do you want to go home, my lad?" Of course, all wanted to and some said so. Festubert was no fit place for boys of 16 and 17 and the majority were sent home. One little boy said in answer to the CO's question: "I should like to go home and see my father and mother, but I think my place is here Sir." For a moment the Colonel hesitated and then said: "Well I am proud of you, my lad." With an eager smile the boy asked: "Am I to stay Sir?" And beamed with delight when the CO said: "Yes."

7329 Pte. John Milton Jones had pleaded with the Colonel to let him stay, and he remained in the Battalion.

On December 14th scarlet fever broke out in 'C' and 'D' Companies and all had to be isolated until the symptoms passed.

On 20th December, in the most miserable of weather, the Battalion left base camp for the small town of Festubert. The rankers were unaware where they were heading and just followed the orders to march. Conditions were wretched for the twenty mile march, the rain beating down ceaselessly. There was one stop in the town of Merville where tea of sorts was brewed, but no sooner had the billy-cans started to warm when the order came to pack up and move on out.

They were now marching south in the wind and rain and the Terriers met on the road an Irish Regiment, and they marched together until 7 a.m., reaching the outskirts of Bethune.

They were exhausted but were surprised when an order came to make ready to attack the enemy!

They were having no chance be bed down or rest. The Battalion was ordered to fix bayonets and stand to. They were at a farm building in the village of Gorre and it began to dawn on the lads that there was a major battle taking place. The noise and the urgency of men rushing around suggested this was serious.

Officially the 4th RWF were now in reserve, behind the main forces of Gloucesters, Welsh Regiment and South Wales Borderers, all three of whom taking a heavy pounding from the Germans.

Pte. Laurie Miller seemed quite offended by this turn of events:

" *We were surprised. We went into the firing line after walking 25 miles without food, and then into the attack.*"

The 4th Battaion were now in the thick of things, war had become serious and it became evident that with casualties of the SWB pouring past them from the front line, they looked likely to be next to into action.

Long day turned into night. The sounds of war were all around them as they huddled in holes and behind walls at a random derelict farm. An order was shout. " *Fix bayonets.*" A whistle shrilled and a Very Light coloured the sky as the men ranked up and then crept forward in the dark of night.

Bullets whizzed by. Lights exploded in the sky. Mud and water sucked at their boots. Every breath was held. A signaller pointed the way to the jump off point from where the Denbigh men would be starting their attack.

A random bullet fizzed, hitting Sergeant J.P. Edwards of the Rhos Company. Two men were assigned to helpe him to the medics in the rear.

The Denbigh boys crept forward along duck-boards when a cry of anguish rang out! Corporal William David Evans, Hennessey Terrace, described what happened:

" *I took Sergeant John Owen Thomas's son Jackie to hospital the night we were getting under fire. He had fallen down a shell hole full of water and was in an awful state ; and in taking him to the rear I nearly lost my lot it was so dark. I soon found them again. What happened was a party of us were advancing to the firing line in single file. As we were moving forward, motor ambulances were coming conveying the wounded from the front line. In getting out of the way, Jackie Thomas fell headlong into this dangerous hole.*"

The men now gathered at the jump off point. They waited and waited. Eventually an order came to 'stand down.'

That was excitement enough. Pte. David Thomas Edwards wrote to his brother, Owen Edwards at Llanrhaeadr Post Office.

"We were ordered, about 30 of us, to take ammunition to the front line. We were under heavy fire and were well praised for it."

There was a lucky escape for two Denbigh men. L/Cpl Eleazer Davies (Leicester Terrace) was stood next to Pte. Edward Hughes of Wesley Place. A strange whizzing noise filled their ears. Something fell out of the sky and landed in a puddle of water a foot or so away. They looked at the German shell and decided between them that it was the water that had rendered it ineffective.

In another part of the line, the Wrexham Company had been fighting for their lives as William Williams of Ruabon wrote:

" *We saw the Germans advancing onto us but we kept pouring heavy fire into their ranks. On the third morning the enemy charged us with the bayonet. But we ran out to meet them. Some ran back but others came on. They outnumbered us two to one I should imagine. There came a fellow at me and tried to thrust his bayonet into my chest. I knocked him off and getting my chance I put my bayonet through his neck. It was his life or mine. I pulled my bayonet out and swung the butt head round at the Hun who was bothering the fellow next to me.*"

William David Evans :

" *Midnight on the 21st December. We are eating the contents of a parcel near to a ruined house, with firing and shelling going on all around us.*"

Relief finally came and the Denbigh Terriers were marched back to Bethune after their exhausting first experience of war. Waiting for them were gifts of tobacco and fags from Buller's, together with post from family and friends. Sergeant Carless wrote to Mr. Buller, the tobacconist on Bridge Street , thanking him for his generosity , for it was he who had sent them on behalf of the town.

Now trench warfare was to be part of the life of the Denbigh boys. Christmas was here and it was like no other for them:

" *For Christmas dinner we had biscuits and jam. So far we have had six wounded and one killed. Feet get frost bitten. And it is not safe to walk about with snipers. We expect to get relief soon. We are with a Lieutenant , a jolly chap who has just handed each of us a far. Wherever he goes , I go also."* signed : David Thomas Edwards.

The man killed was 24 year old 7508 Pte. Elwy Hughes of Llangollen. He was killed on Christmas Eve by a shell exploding over the trench. He was the first of the 'Fighting Fourth' killed in action.

By this date over 100 officers and men had been invalided home due to frostbite and rheumatism , including the Dr. J.C. Davies , Captain of the Rhos Company of the 4th RWF. He had been one of the oldest volunteers.

William David Evans : *" I may tell you that my Christmas Day was a very dreary one in a trench. My dinner was a few biscuits and water , so you may bet that I was happy with bullets flying about! But they have not managed to hit me yet. We had a piece of plum pudding on Boxing Day , it was what the Daily News sent out. And we had Princess Mary's gift , a very nice box of tobacco and a Christmas Card from the King and Queen. I can tell you that 1915 came in while we were in the trenches."*

The Kaiser's Birthday

And so 1915 started as 1914 ended, with the Terriers now occupying the trenches in rotation with other Regiment Battalions in the Brigade. Shelling and sniping continued unabated, if at a rather less frenetic pace.

The 4th RWF were in and around the village of Givenchy, what is now a picturesque and pleasant place. Back in 1915 it was anything but peaceful.

The British had some success of their own with shelling the enemy in retaliation as Corporal Thomas Roberts of Henllan Street explained : " *I saw a shell heave the earth up and a German thrown into the air and fall stone dead. We take a few pot shots but I don't know is we polish any off.*"

Quality information was slow in reaching loved ones back home in Denbighshire. Rumours swept the town that the Terriers had been decimated in a German assault, the news becoming mixed up with that of the 1st Battalion RWF who had suffered serve losses. The casualty figues of the winter war were only now coming to light. The 1st Battalion were so short of Officers that Captain Minshull Ford was transferred to take command of this Line Battalion. His replacement as adjutant was Major Cyril Frankland Meares of the Royal Irish Fusiliers.

Pte. Joe Wilson of the Green wrote that he was in hospital with frostbite. Pte. T. Godfrey Edwards was being treated for pneumonia in Cambridge. James Gilmore of Henllan Street was also suffering with frostbite. The weather continued to account for most of the casualties.

Pte. David Davies, a veteran of 12 years service with the Terriers, was in Wooton Hospital with shrapnel wounds to his legs. Pte. John Roberts of Henllan Street was in hospital in Rouen with deafness due to 'cannonading' and Walter Davies, Factory Place, had been shot in the arm. Wallace Roberts was home after being shot in the leg and had been in the same Liverpool hospital ward as Pte. Ellis Williams, a fellow Terrier.

The 19th Bengal Lancers relieved the Terriers and it gave the men chance to write home.

Reg Lewis :

" *We have been in the trenches for 17 days and have just come from there for a rest. But we expect to go back any time now. I hope you don't believe what you hear about us in town as we have not been cut up as people think we have. Indeed I think we have been very lucky, as we have been as close as 300 yards to the Germans.*"

Pte. Lincoln Miller wrote from Beckett's Park Hospital, Leeds. This goes to explain the conditions the Denbigh men had to endure and which was responsible for the number of men invalided home :

" *I must thank God for what He has brought me through these past seventeen days – shells and bullets passing my head from all parts of the line. Just think of me within 200 yards of the Germans. I have stood up to my loins in water for the past 17 days.*"

Trench foot was another curse afflicting the British army in general and the Terriers in particular, and it was not until, whale oil was introduced that the problem subsided a little.

The whale oil needed to be rubbed into the feet three times a day (this was stringently enforced) and when in the summer of 1915 long boots replaced puttees in wet conditions (puttees were subsequently used officially for marching and home service only , though in desert campaigns and on the Somme their use continued in most units) the problem reduced significantly after the winter of 1915.

Shell shock was a new phenomena for the medics - and particularly the War Office- to contend with. It took two years before it was truly accepted as a medical condition and was initially considered as a malingering illness. What is surprising is that comparatively few few suffered with it , despite thousands of front line soldiers undergoing bombardments often on a daily basis.

Colonel France-Hayhurst noted that the men seemed very down after spending 17 days in the trenches but thought they had brightened up considerably after three days out. *"The regime became normalised , three days in , three out. Weather conditions were abnormally bad, the snow and floods precluding any active operations during the first three weeks of January."* (Sir John French) .

It was approaching the Kaiser's birthday , 25th January , and the Germans intended to celebrate with a ferocious attack on the Allied lines. The Terriers were to feel the full force of their action whilst in the trenches at La Bassee lez Givenchy.

On the morning of the attack , the Germans shelled the front trench and forced the British and Indian forces to retreat. Once the shelling ceased the Germans attacked.

Pte. Joseph Kent explained what happened from a local point of view :

" On the 24th , the Germans shelled our trenches all day and all night , killing and wounding many of our men. They were trying to find our guns but could not do so . The armoured train behind us would send them a few shells over , then go back so that the Germans could not find it. They charged early in the morning , thinking we had emptied our trenches , but our boys were waiting for them."

Pte. Albert Edward Myddleton :

" The battle began at 7.25 in the morning and they made a charge at us all along the line. The trench had 400 on the right and 50 on the left. The Germans took one trench from us but we got it back in an hour's time and gained 100 yards. The shells were dropping everywhere around us."

Lieutenant Brian Croom-Johnson , along with two other officers and some men retook the trench without casualty and taking 35 prisoners , including two German officers.

The shelling was not just aimed at the trenches. Another target was the canal lock in order to flood the British lines. The Germans had now advanced over a canal and were swarming through the village of Givenchy. Fierce fighting lasted for hours until one or the other side had to give.

Sergeant Evan J. Lake:

" *We were in the trenches when the Germans shelled us for an hour and a half. Then the order came to retire, it was so bad. Very nearly all our fellows were buried alive by the bombardment, so what little was spared we retired to the village close by. Then at a given signal the Germans advanced in thousands so we were reinforced by The Black Watch and went into the attack, and there an awful scene occurred. The dead were lying in their hundreds on the battlefield – both German and our own men.*"

The 4th RWF were occupying two trenches.

Lt.Colonel France Hayhurst:

" *'Scottish Trench' held 50 men under the command of Lt. Hazeldene. This trench ran 50 yards long. The Germans made several attempts to reach the trench but failed. 'Welsh Trench' under Lt. Johnson and 40 RWF men occupying 40 yards, the rest of this trench being occupied by the Welch Regiment. This trench was evacuated and after the shelling ceased was regained and all the enemy in it prisoners. The RWF Machine Gun was in this trench.*"

One Company of 4th RWF was held in reserve. This company took part in the counter attack under Captain T.O.Bury, and also reinforced Scottish Trench.

William David Evans :

" *We were shelled out of our trench so we had to get out and get another position. Well, we let them come up to a certain place, then made a counter attack and took the trench back with a great many prisoners.*"

An Australian eyewitness spoke of scattered parties of Germans virtually annihilated after they had passed over the Allied trenches and entered the village. The British machine guns also swept the main road into Givenchy down which hundreds of the enemy attacked. The Australian wrote that German dead littered the ground.

Pte. Joseph Kent :

" *After charging five times they gave it up and I can tell you that they lost heavily. We took a lot of prisoners, most of whom had been wounded by our shrapnel. We walked alongside some of them and they were quite happy, smoking. This was the charge which Sergeant Ledsham made his name for saving the gun.*"

Lance Sergeant Ledsham earned the Distinguished Conduct Medal and was cited later in the London Gazette as follows :

" *3220 L/Sgt. W. Ledsham, 4th Bn., RWF. (Denbighshire). TF. (LG 30/6/15). For conspicuous gallantry at Givenchy on 25th January 1915. After affording gallant support to an officer in his attack on a trench under heavy fire, he unearthed a buried machine gun, mounted it and opened fire on the enemy*"

The official summary of his gallant conduct stated '*On the 25th January, 1915, during an attack by the Germans at Givenchy-La-Basse, he gallantly led a section under heavy fire to* clear some buildings occupied by Germans. Later, on the retaking of a section of trench which had been captured by the enemy, he displayed great initiative in remounting a machine gun, temporarily dismantled, and keeping up fire on the German position until wounded by a shell from a trench mortar.' He had been with the Territorials for 16 years.

William David Evans :

" *I was in the charge with the Black Watch. My word, I do not know how I got through it, but all the same I did, and I and a few others took 35 prisoners in the trench. All the damage I had that day was that I had my great coat ripped by a piece of shrapnel. The shell burst quite near me. I thought my end had come, but when the shock died away I found myself still alive.*"

It was the first time in the war that the Scots pipers played troops into action.

Another Fusilier wrote:

" *We were at La Bassee when we regained the trench lost by the Indians, and we held them – a very trying experience. We were behind the South Wales Borderers, who had run short of ammunition, so it was up to us to take it. Some took ammunition, others worked as stretcher bearers. It was a very risky job.*"

Lt.Col. France-Hayhurst :

" *Lt. Rouffignac and 50 men held part of New Cut Trench. The village was successfully held and the Brigade was congratulated by Sir John French and Corps Commander. The 4th RWF also received the congratulations of the Brigadier.*"

After it was over, it was time to count the cost. Denbigh had lost two men.

Pte. John Price Thomas. Jack Thomas to those who knew him. He was twenty years of age and the son of William Thomas, postman. Jack was also a postman and his memory is retained on a plaque in Denbigh Post Office. Jack was a footballer with Denbigh Town FC and said to be one of the finest half backs in North Wales.

Not long before his death he had written home saying he did not feel like coming home until he had finished his work fighting for his country. His brother, William 'Bill' Thomas, was aboard the H.M.S. Colossus and Sergeant Evan Lake wrote to him about his brother's death.

" *Jack and I charged together and sorry to say Jack was shot dead. He died like a hero amongst friends. God's Will be done.*"

Another letter from Sergeant Lake gave more detail on how his young friend died.

" *Jack, Will Evans and I were close together and we were going back to the trenches we had just lost. Jack's rifle jammed and he got up on his knees to see what the matter was. The fierce fighting had ceased. We had won and taken a lot of prisoners. We were glad and got up to have a smoke. But one of the wretched Germans had hidden himself in a ruined church close by to us. No one dreamed there were any of them left. So the man came up on the sly and unfortunately poor old Jack was the first to rise and the man fired and killed Jack stone* dead through his head. He had also killed three of the Scotchmen before we could get to him as he was well covered. But when we did get hold of him, the Scotchmen cut him to pieces."

Evan Lake was deeply upset, enough to put himself in danger:

" *Will Evans and myself carried Jackie to a cemetery 700 yards off, through all the deadly fire. I did not care if I was killed myself as we could be buried together. His last words were of home.*

Well I am alone now, lost both Jack and Tom Davies who is wounded. We three were never parted since we left Northampton before until that awful morning. I have got all Jack's things so if there is a chance of sending them, I will – if not gone myself"

After burial, Sergeant Lake planted a crucifix and some everlasting flowers and wrote some words upon the grave:

" *Here lies a gallant hero, Jack Price Thomas of Denbigh.* "

Corporal Thomas Roberts of 104 Henllan Street was also killed. In civilian life Thomas was a tailor at Bradleys, Denbigh. A native of Ruthin, he was a married man with six children.

Evan Lake :

" *Tom Roberts was just on the left of Jackie and I, so he lived to reach the trenches again. You know, we have duties to do in the trenches and he was the first to go and look out, so he got up to start and was shot twice by a sniper. He did not speak a word after and was buried on the spot, poor man.*"

Sergeant Carless:

" *Young J.P.Thomas went under, also Corporal T. Roberts. They did as good as the best, we are sorry to lose them, but it is the fortunes of war. We don't know whose turn it is next.* "

Pte. Albert Edward Myddleton :

" *Corporal Thomas Roberts of Henllan Street (was) killed in the trench on Monday 25*[th] *January. He was shot in the head and heart. Also Pte. John Price Thomas, who was shot in the head on the same day.*"

Others in the 4th RWF killed in the action were Edward Evans (Wrexham), William Fail (He lived in St.Helens and was born in Rhos), W.H. Tomkins (Wrexham), John Griffiths (Wrexham), Edward Morgan (Wrexham), Charles Stokes (Chirk), Albert Prescott, Edwin Jones, W. Higgins (Wrexham), and Lt. John Arthur Hughes (St. Asaph).

Lt. John Arthur Hughes was a solicitor who trained in Denbigh, lived in St. Asaph and worked in Ruthin. He was described as good company, having a happy disposition and being an excellent singer.

One report states : " *He was proceeding down a communication trench leading to the fire trench and seeing an officer lying outside the trench , apparently wounded , he got out of the communication trench to render assistance. He found the officer already dead and in returning to his men was shot in two places. He died of his wounds two days later."*

Dr. Johnson of the 3rd Field Ambulance wrote : " *He lost his life in saving another. One of his men was wounded and he got out of the trench and dragged the man in. As he was getting in himself he was shot by a rifle bullet. All who attended him were struck by his bravery in his last hours."*

John Arthur Hughes had been gazetted on 3rd October 1914 along with Thomas Reinnallt Williams (Llewsog) and Douglas Craig-Johnson as 2/Lts in 4th RWF.

He is buried in Bethune Town Cemetery.

After the rage of battle , the Germans were not giving any quarter to their enemies. Pte. William Clayton and Pte. John Robert Riley were two of the youngest in 'D' Company and they were employed as stretcher bearers. This proved hazardous work.

Pte. Joseph Kent :

"Every time we went out that day to bring in our wounded , shells were dropping all around us. They would not let up."

Pte. Albert Edward Myddleton:

" *The sight of the battlefield was terrible and would make you drop down if you saw the bodies , some of the British , some of them German , the place being black with them. It was a proper slaughter and as you were pushing forward you could not help treading on the dead."*

There were plenty of wounded. Corporal Eleazer Davies (Asylum Staff) wrote stoically to his wife from hospital:

" *I received a wound from a shell bursting outside a brick wall and it blew the wall up. The bricks struck me above the right eye knocking me down five yards. The remainder of the wall then fell on me , injuring my right arm. I was then unconscious."*

Also wounded were Pte. Edward Wright (Beacon's Hill) , Pte. Thomas John Davies (Penybanc Cottage) , Pte. Edward Jones (Tower Terrace) , Pte. John W. Jones and Pte William Parry , an asylum attendant whose wounds were so severe that he was to succumb to them later in the war. Eventually invalided out of the army , William is one of thousands who died 'out of khaki' and therefore not shown on official army death lists. He is buried in Henllan Churchyard.

Pte. Ted Jones was sent to the Duchess of Westminster Hospital and was with the wounded visited by the Prince of Wales. Sergeant Carless was also wounded and sent to hospital.

On Sunday evening , 6th February , a service of Remembrance was held in St. Mary's to honour Jack Price Thomas and Thomas Roberts. The whole of the Post Office staff in Denbigh came, and the church was packed with townspeople. The Rev. W. Gabriel Evans and Rev. David Thomas officiated in this service which was conducted in Welsh. The service finished with the 'Death March' played by organist W. Pierce. Some of the family members had to be helped home, such was their sorrow.

Two brothers in the Battalion, Walter and Edward Lloyd (sons of Mr. Cadwaladr Lloyd of Nantglyn), were both involved in the battle. Walter was in hospital soon after with pneumonia. Edward continued at the front.

Pte. Arthur Lewis, one of three brothers in the 4th RWF wrote home.

" I left Warrie when we came down to Marles les Mines for a rest, but as for Reg I cannot tell you where he is now, as I left him in hospital in France, so I told Warren to buck up and do his best in the fighting as I too have been sent to hospital."

Marles les Mines was a coal-mining town 5 miles south of Bethune. The smell of coal was everywhere and slag heaps darkened the already gloomy horizon. Soldiers were now bivouacked in fields, sheltered in the few remaining billets or shoved into railway sidings.

Pte. Meredydd Ellis, Panton Hall, was wounded. He was also suffering with rheumatism after long periods in the rain and snow, that seemed to be never ending.

" I was then sent to hospital in Bethune, in France and then moved to four other hospitals. Then they packed us all on a train. We were travelling two days and two nights, then reached Le Havre. We crossed on the hospital ship 'Asturias' to Southampton."

The 'HMHS Asturias' was hit by a torpedo in February 1915 but did not sink. It was attacked again in 1917 and ran aground with loss of life.

Captain W.C.B.Williams, commanding D Company, wrote to his parents in Llewesog Hall:

" The Battalion were in action on 26th and did well. There were casualties, telve killed and 28 wounded. Gronwy Griffith was wounded in the leg after good work with the machine gun. Lieutenant Hughes died of wounds."

Despite all that had happened, one man described his feelings about being away from his mates.

Pte. Arthur Lewis :

" I will be glad when I am better and able to go back to Warren and the boys at the front."

Neuve Chapelle

With the Battalion now heading for Marles les Mines for some well deserved rest, it may be a good opportunity to look at some aspects of the war in more detail.

To start off, it must be remembered that the 'Tommy' had no idea what the state of play was in any area except in his own immediate trench. Most quality information reaching the public was from soldiers lying in hospital beds in 'Blighty' and not from those in the front line, as letters and postcards were now becoming rigorously censored.

History tells us that the situation on the Western Front was stalemate. History also tells us that 'pushes' such as we have seen at La Bassee against those defending resulted in heavy casualties suffered by the aggressors.

The Germans seemed to have learned this sharp lesson from their action some called ' The Kaisers's Birthday Attack' as from that moment we see the Allies taking the role of aggressor and the Germans concentrating on defending what they had.

They now started to fall back until they were on higher ground, and began constructing substantial and well fortified trench systems. These contained concrete bunkers, underground passages and thick wire entanglements.

The Germans created a three trench system that became difficult to break through. There were only a handful of men in the forward trench., with more gathered in the support trench and the majority of their soldiers in the reserve trench. The reserve trench was dug deep into the earth and reinforced with concrete.

To be fair to General -Later Field Marshall- Haig, he stated early in the war that the Germans would have to be worn down and that losses would be heavy on both sides. That proved to be the consequence of expert German defence together with the under-rated machine gun.

France had asked the British to help relieve their situation back in December, and another request was coming for help by making another attack to distract the Germans who were giving the French a torrid time. It was pressure to bear and digging substantial trenches of their own was not on the agenda of the UK military high command.

So whilst the enemy concentrated his attention on defence, the Allies got ready to attack. And that spelt consequences for the men from Denbigh.

The reserve depot of the 4th RWF was in Abbey Road, Cambridge under the command of Colonel Edgar John Swayne (Solicitor). Men to replace those coming back to Blighty by the shipload were all but drying up. Where were all the Denbighites and why weren't they 'doing their bit'? Adverts began to appear in the local press in Denbigh urging men to do their patriotic duty and step forward to join the Territorials in France and Flanders. Letters from unnamed persons and articles with such titles as ' A Woman Has Her Say', in which young men were urged in the most heart rending terms to join the battle, began to appear in the local papers.

There was already a huge recruitment campaign and the 4th RWF had to compete with rthe Royal Artillery, the Welsh Army Service Corps, the new Pals Battalions and other neighbouring County Battalions for fresh blood.

Councillors were also doing their bit in pushing the young men of Denbigh to the war. One took it upon himself to visit houses in the town and take an unofficial poll of all the men of service age not in khaki. This caused a bout of ill feeling in the town. Men were of course joining the colours. Joe Kearns enlisted as soon as he came of age. Llewelyn Thomas (Preswhylfa) joined the Yeomanry and his brother Peter the Royal Fusiliers in London.

It took a personal intervention by means of an open letter from Colonel France Hayhurst to reassure the families of Denbigh that the town was pulling its weight.

Denbigh's leaders suffered as any family of Denbigh was to suffer. The Mayor Mr. Dryhurst Roberts lost a son in 1917. The Town Clerk, Mr. Edward Parry, lost a son in Mesopotamia. Denbigh's Member of Parliament also lost a son. This gradually led him to take a rather unfashionable anti-war stance which cost him his seat in 1918.

Cambridge men were being drafted into the Battalion just in time for the Terriers to take their places back in the trenches.

On 25th February they were stationed at Essars and on 1st March the Battalion celebrated St. David's Day.

Official Records:

"St David's Day on 1 March 1915. All ranks wore leeks in their caps and during the officers' dinner a borrowed goat, with horns painted gold was led around the table accompanied by a drummer playing a biscuit tin."

John Jones, 14 Brookhouse Mill:

" The nights are cold. We are all back in again after the rest and new clothing which was needed. We have new high boots as the snow is up to our knees in places. We also got fur coats which are very warm. There are sad sights here, with houses and churches burnt to the ground. The dead are lying all around and it is not possible to bury them. We are 48 hours in, 48 hours out."

The 4th RWF were now occupying a new trench near the town of Festubert. At the end of February Captain Freddie Clough returned to the front line and a new Officer 2nd Lieutenant Francis Graham Evans, the son of the Vicar of Llanrhaeadr. Sergeant Carless was promoted to Lieutenant. Sergeant John Henry Emmanuel was promoted to Company Sergeant Major. He was back home in charge of musketry in Northampton. Sgt.John Pierce Jones, stationed in Bedford, was promoted to Sergeant Major.

There was not much way in comfort out of the front line. Some had not seen a proper bed since July but had to make do with dug outs in the ground.

Sergeant William David Davies:

" *We cannot get any house to billet in as they have all been shelled to the ground. There is not a house up for miles around here. When we first went up to the trenches here, we were up to our knees in water and we had to do the best we could. We had to put some boards down and sleep on them. Our Captain and all had to do so – he is Captain Clough. All the men like him as he is for fair play with the men. He is with us in the firing line and with the men all day."*

Captain F. Clough :

" *Our boys are grand, perfectly cool in the trenches, happy, good tempered, you can do nothing but love them, they are so grand and cheerful under the circumstances."*

The next test was on 10th March, the Battle of Neuve Chapelle. There 4th RWF were on stand by only for this action. General Haig wanted to test the German resolve for a bigger offensive later in the year. The Terriers watched on their right side of the trench as the battle unfolded. On occasions the Germans launched at their trench and had to be repulsed by the machine gun. Five Wrexham men were killed by shell fire. And the third day of battle resulted in more casualties.

Captain F. B. Clough:

" *I am so tired I can hardly write. We have just done a week in the trenches in the firing line, the German trenches being about 200 yards away from us. I am sorry to say that we had five killed and twelve wounded including an officer. I nearly had it twice. A shell cut a tree in half in front of me and a shot hit the trench just above my head."*

6775 Pte. John (Johnny) Parry was killed on 9th March.

Pte. John Milton Jones, the boy who refused to go home, was killed on the 10th March.

L/Cpl Thomas Jones of Coedpoeth on 11th March.

Miner David John Jones of Bersham died on 13th March. 6069 L/Cpl John Lloyd of Acrefair died of wounds on 10th March.

Those wounded included the following :

7433 L/Cpl William Hughes of 8 Wesley Place. He was wounded in the hand. He had a finger removed. His brother Ted stayed in the trenches as Will was shipped home. Will wrote from hospital that Ted had *'killed a good lot of Germans.'*

L/Cpl Richard Pritchard of 133 Henllan Street. He would be wounded several more times during the war.

Thomas Myddleton Jones who had arrived in January from Cambridge wrote to his friend Howell Tudor Hughes of Bronallt:

" *I was on observation duty with Sergeant Major Wainwright during the greatest bombardment ever known in history, 10th March."*

The number of shells used in the bombardment, which lasted 35 minutes, exceeded the total used in the whole of the Boer War.

Thomas Myddleton Jones:

" *We were awaiting the signal to reinforce our men. Hat day I shall never forget and really it is a shame to say, but the Artillery mowed them down like sheep. It was a pretty sight, shells falling in their trenches and the poor fellows that were left were mad."*

The call to reinforce never came.. The British had taken a beating despite the bombardment and Haig called off the attack after casualty figures began to mount.

Sergeant William David Davies:

" *It would be a sight for you to see the place after this big battle. There is hardly a tree standing that has not been damaged by shells. There is not a house standing up here. There was a house between us and the German trench and it was very handy for their snipers. So our guns had a shot at it and it was cleared to the ground after five shells.* "

Captain F.B.Clough:

" *Think of us poor chaps here and risking our lives and going through a regular hell of it. I cannot give you in writing the whole hellish murder that is going on. But I can say that the sooner we send more men over, the sooner the whole devilish story will be over."*

After the battle was over some of the Denbigh men of the 4th Battalion met up with others from the town serving in other regiments near to the battle front.

Sergeant Major George Wainwright, who had been out since November without leave or injury met Sergeant J.G. Lloyd of Leicester Terrace. Sgt. Lloyd was serving with the South Wales Borderers. Sgt. Lloyd's brother, Pte.D.O.Lloyd was working at the Base Hospital in Bethune in the Royal Army Medical Corps. He was seen and had a conversation with Denbigh casualties John Caledfryn Davies and Edward Wright. John Caledfryn was the brother of two other serving men, Walter and Thomas Albert Davies.

Robert William Ellis of 'A' Company in the 4th RWF met with Thomas H. Myddleton of the 1st RWF. Also he spoke with Edward Heber Jones of the Royal Field Artillery. By the 21st April, Edward Heber Jones was dead, killed at Fauquissart whilst carrying a German shell which exploded in his hands, a fragment entering his heart.

On 14th March the Terriers were relieved by the 1st Bn. Northamptonshire Regt and marched to Long Cornet near the town of Bethune for a rest.

On the 24th March they were back on the battle field at Neuve Chapelle. The weather was beginning to improve.

William David Evans:

" *The weather is much better now , but frosty at night. We are now on a part of the front line where we gained a great victory a short time ago. These has been an awful slaughter here and I should like you to see some of the damage done in the villages. There is a church near our lines in ruins and in the cemetery the only thing standing is a large wooden crucifix. The whole place looks as if an earthquake has taken place. In the trenches we hold we are treading on dead Germans with very little earth over them . I suppose many were buried alive during the bombardment."*

Lance Corporal Edward Jones (Ted Muir) of 10 Henllan Street:

"It is a queer sensation to be under fire for the first time. The noise of the shells , bullets and bombs make you realise that you are taking part in the war of wars. I am in the next dug out to William Evans in our present trench and I see a great deal of him."

William David Evans:

" *We are all proud of Arthur Jones of Saron , he gives us and the Huns plenty of old Welsh songs and hymns. Indeed , he and Cpl. Edward Hughes and Elias Albert Jones make a fine trio!"*

Pte. Reg Lewis:

" *We get many a bit of fun in the trenches. We shout at the Germans and they do likewise and they start calling us all sorts of names ; then it finishes off with ten rounds of rapid fire!"*

There were dangerous duties to perform. According to William David Davies there were now only nine out of the original sixty seven Denbigh lads still out at the front. Pte. Thomas Myddleton Jones described what was expected of soldiers in the front line:

"I have been out all night with a fatigue party between both lines supporting our communication trench , but we had to keep quite silent. We lost one comrade , Harry Clarke from Ruthin , who died of his wound poor chap , just as we were coming out of a wood and it is a wonder we did not lose more. We had to return before time because a German listening patrol was out. Captain Lloyd has been sent to hospital totally run down , but we expect him back in a few days time and we miss him very much."

One of the most important tasks facing the men was to make the trench more hospitable and to supplement the structure , in most cases by breastworks make of bricks and sandbags. The routine in the trenches during the tour was that a platoon would spend two days in the front line trench , the 'firing line', and two days in a support trench. Of the two , it was the support trench which often proved most dangerous , as the enemy shelled it more frequently as they knew it held most of the men.

The changeovers would occur at night under the cover of darkness for secrecy. Dawn would be the period to be alert for a German assault and about half an hour before it became light everyone would 'stand to'. As soon as it was light enough to see, then men got down to cleaning their rifles. After inspection by a Sergeant it was time to get more sleep up until breakfast, which was brought up at 630am. The men were then put to work after nine o'clock rebuilding damage to the trench and breastworks with sandbags. Lookouts were posted in the forward 'sap' and these were changed as the day & night progressed. The 'sap' was the furthest point to the enemy lines and was occupied by two soldiers. They would watch for enemy movement and report any finding back down the line. The main danger to them were snipers and so periscopes were used to observe.

The forward trench was rarely dug in a straight line, so as to stop the enemy from firing straight into the defenders if part of the trench was taken. The firebay was the forward part of the trench, the traverse was the rear. The communication trench was also dug in zigzag pattern. A communication trench was dug from an old front line trench to a new captured trench. Often these communication trenches were hundreds of yards long and change of personnel was processed through them.

Dinner was at noon followed by a rest period until 4 o'clock. Tea was followed by more work and rest. T 7 o'clock rifles were cleaned and inspected again. At 730pm all had to 'stand to'. Some worked well into midnight and were rewarded with soup.

The breakfast for the men would be something like a slice of stale bread and a slice of bacon. Dinner would be bully beef boiled in pea soup with either a dried biscuit or a piece of bread. There were lots of potatoes and onions which the men fried up, each having a different method of cooking their meal. The main food grumble was lack of choice. There was a rum ration and was usually preserved for those returning from night patrol or any good works deemed rewarding.

Night parties went out to cut wire, gather intelligence, fix the wire and on occasions to raid the enemy in order to capture a prisoner.

On 27th March, 6397 Pte. Harold Harrison Jones of Glanrafon, Llandyrnog was killed and two days later 7533 Pte. Robert Owen Hughes of Saron was shot stone dead by a sniper whilst digging. Neither of these has a known grave. Their names appear on the Le Touret Memorial

Captain F.B.Clough wrote of them in his letter home:

" *In the last trenches I am sorry to say that young Hughes of Saron and Jones, late of Llandyrnog were killed. A great loss. They were such quiet lads. Our Company Sergeant Major R.H.Jones of Ruthin was also wounded but is getting on well and wishes to be back with us again. This is the sort of grand spirit our men are showing.*"

Whilst resting in Chocques, the men of 'D' Company received a gift from Mr. Evan Jones, newsagent and tobacconist. He had sent 150 packets of cigarettes, each pack containing five fags. Letters were also an important boost for the men a long way from home.

Pte. Thomas Myddleton Jones:

"*My wish is always in our short intervals to answer letters from home and elsewhere, which do encourage one's hearts whilst out here: letters are most acceptable.*"

By the end of April Captain Clough had left the front line action and returned home, struck down again with rheumatism. The Battalion now moved to a trench system called Rue de L'Epinette whch they shared with the Black Watch and more exotic troops.

Thomas Myddleton Jones:

" *The Gurkhas and Indians are amongst us, they are fine chaps and I can tell you they have no mercy for the enemy and the knife goes flying around them. Awful chaps they are, death or glory, they are proud to die on the battlefield. The Black Watch have done well and saved us many a time.*"

One night a burly Watchman was sharing guard duty with a small Welsh Terrier.

" *What Battalion are you with, then?*" growled the Scotsman.

" *4^h Royal Welsh...Saturday soldiers!*" responded the cocky Welshman.

" *Well, you're on bloody overtime now!*"

Death Comes On Aubers Ridge

The 9th May was memorable inasmuch that the first troops of Kitchener's New Army left Britain for service in France. Whilst these fresh faced volunteers were gathering, General Haig was determined to capture ground at Aubers Ridge in a prelude to a sustained attack and hopeful breakthrough at the town of Festubert.

After Neuve Chapelle, Haig was convinced that a sustained bombardment followed by a huge infantry push would break the German line. The objective was to break through the enemy's lines on the La Bassee-Lille road between La Bassee and Fournes. The 1st Division were ordered to attack from behind it's breastworks in front of the Rue du Bois. Two cavalry units were in reserve to exploit successes.

On the evening of the 8th, the Battalion were ordered to parade and march. They arrived near to the front line at midday. The 4th Battalion RWF settled themselves behind some breastworks and listened to a bombardment which began at 5 a.m. that lasted 45 minutes. They were fully kitted out, packed full of equipment and clothing, despite the warm weather.

The Fusilier wore a Balaclava helmet, a muffler, overcoat, tunic, shirt, cardigan, trousers, braces, body belt, socks and boots.

He carried a rifle fixed with a bayonet. Attached to him was an entrenching tool, ammo pouches left and right, a water bottle, a small knapsack, a hip knife and a haversack on his back.

Within the haversack were the following : cigarettes, matches, tinder lighter, two pipes, khaki handkerchief, an ounce of tobacco, a small knife, a pencil, a purse with a few coppers or francs, a pair of scissors, grocery ration of biscuit and bully, tea tablets, roll book, knife and fork, a spoon, an enamel mug. Also a compass, a bar of soap, a toothbrush, razor and leather case for razor blades. A first aid tin containing iodine and a bandage. Sometimes a waterproof sheet but not today. The personal belongings of the man, letters, dress uniform, personal possessions were stored at the Base Camp at Hinges.

L/Sgt Charles Carrington sent five Belgian pennies home and wrote in a letter to his wife :

"We have had three weeks' rest, and we had some fine weather out here, but we are going up to the trenches tonight and I pray to God that He will pull me through this for once. Glad to tell you that all the boys are all right, but our hearts are at home".

Pte.N.N.Jones:

"The clergy were waiting for us on the road. They prayed with us. It was impressive. The barrage started at 4.am. There were hundreds of guns. It made you tremble."

At 5.45 am. the barrage stopped and an eerie silence made the ears sing. Whistles started to sound along the trenches that seemed to stretch left and right for miles. The Officer in charge of the 4th RWF looked at his pocket watch. He replaced the timepiece back into his top pocket and drew his hand gun. With his left hand he raised his whistle to his lips, looked left and right, and after a second's pause he blew. The Battle for Aubers Ridge had begun.

Pte.N.N.Jones.

" I am in the first section and twenty of us had to cross a field to get to our trenches, well I went like a shot. I lost my friend Millington the first few yards. He was shot through the side close by me."

Sergeant William David Davies :

" At the start of the fight our Colonel was shouting at us to lead on. He was the first over and he was shot down. He died a quiet death with no pain at all. We lost our officer Lieutenant Croom-Johnson. He also had a quiet death. Ted Williams of Brynffynnon was wounded in the mouth when going down to help a wounded man , but not very badly thankfully."

After the bombardment had stopped , the Germans had a nasty surprise waiting for Haig's army slowly walking on open ground towards them. The Germans on the ridge rose from their shelters , and set up their machine guns. A Prussian Officer had this to say:

" This solid wall of khaki men , British and Indian side by side. There was only one possible order to give. Fire until the barrels burst!"

Pte. Edward Hughes:

" It was awful and the bombardment was like that at Neuve Chapelle but we had to charge this time."

William David Davies :

" If you could have seen us , it would have made you mad to hear about 1500 guns going off behind your head. Then we had to do the charge twice. The Germans had about 20 maxim guns on us and we had to retreat with heavy losses."

L/Cpl Edward Jones:

" Our Brigade was ordered to attack the German trenches after a heavy bombardment by our artillery which commenced at 5 o'clock in the morning. Our Battalion played a prominent role in the assault , attacking twice the enemy trenches and I am sorry to say paid a heavy price for their bravery with a rather heavy casualty list – about 80 men and 7 officers including the Colonel who was killed leading the attack."

William David Davies:

" Warrie Lewis , Reg's brother , did some fine work. He went to fetch three wounded men under a hail of bullets and shells and brought them safe to the trench. He was lucky not to be hit. He knew that Reg was out wounded somewhere , so Warrie went to look for him and brought him back with three more. They say he has been recommended for the V.C. There are also 3 or 4 more in for the V.C. After that fight."

Reg Lewis had found his way to the German trenches and fought hand to hand with the enemy, but retired with a wound through his arm from a German bayonet.

L/Cpl Edward Jones:

" It was a sickening sight to see them fall and hear them groaning and harder still to go on without being able to render any assistance. On that bit of ground we were exposed to murderous fire from their German maxims and it is a wonder that any of us managed to cross at all."

Pte. Edward Hughes:

" We had to charge across an open field, right through the German line. Ted Myddleton, Reggie Lewis, Teddy Williams, Will Evans and Frank Atkinson were wounded and one of our officers Lieutenant Croom-Johnson was killed. Number 7 platoon lost 12 killed."

L/Cpl Edward Jones:

" Our Doctor (Pern) was killed whilst attending our wounded and he had dressed a number of men when he was hit. He was very brave."

Pte. L.Mitchell, 24th Field Ambulance:

" For three days we never stopped dressing the wounded men as they were brought in and at the end of those three days we still had sixty or seventy stretcher cases outside. I never saw any attack with so many men who had bullet wounds as at Aubers Ridge. The Germans just mowed them down and most of the bullet wounds were through the legs."

Pte.N.N.Jones:

" It was like a butcher's shop – blood and dead everywhere – and so hot the doctors and stretcher bearers could not get near us. Some went only with rifle and bayonet, in short sleeves."

After the first assault failed, a second attempt was ordered for 4pm. Major Cyril Frankland Meares, now the highest ranking officer in the Battalion after the death of Colonel France-Hayhurst, led the remains of the 4th Battalion down a communication trench instead of approaching the German lines in the open. Shells and bullets fell all around them and eventually they ran out of trench and were faced with emerging on an open grassy bank. Before they climbed out and over to the face the German guns once more, an order arrived cancelling the attack. Haig had received casualty returns and they were horrific.

The Records of the Royal Welsh Fusiliers 1914-1919 :

" The 4th Battalion, waiting behind the support line of breastworks for their first plunge into battle, started, on the hour of assault, to cross the first line over the open. But the volume of fire directed on the assaulting troops and sweeping across flat country, was such that they never succeeded in reaching the first line. There was a second assault at 4pm, Major Meares being in command." There were over 11000 British casualties, with no ground won and no advantage gained.

The casualties for the 4th RWF were:

Lt.Colonel Frederick Charles France-Hayhurst of Bostock Hall, Davenham, the son of Colonel Charles Hosken France-Hayhurst (a veteran of the Crimean War). He was killed immediately whilst leading his men on the first charge.

Lieutenant Brian Croom-Johnson was severely wounded in the charge and died of wounds later that day. He was the youngest son of Mr. Harry Croom-Johnson J.P. of The Elms, Wrexham. In civilian live, Lieutenant Croom- Johnson was an Assistant Engineer at the Wrexham and Denbighshire Waterworks Company.

Second Lieutenant John Turner Clough Hazledine aged 39, Burlton Hall, Shrewsbury.

Captain John Eric Evans died of wounds at 1a.m. on 10th May. He was the son of Dr. Evans J.P. Of Wrexham. He had been with the Territorials for six years and was a medical student.

Lieutenant Montague Pern LRCP, MRCS of the RAMC attached 4th RWF was killed treating the wounded in an open field, devoid of any cover. He was 26 years of age. He was from Botley, Hants and had trained at Guy's Hospital.

James MacFarlane (RAMC) wrote:

"We lost one of our Officers on the 9th; he was doing M.O. for the 4th Royal Welsh Fusiliers. He was a splendid chap but a shell did it."

L/Cpl Walter Denson died of wounds. He was from Summerhill, Wrexham.

Pte. William Hughes of Rhosddu.

Lance Corporal John Millington of Rhosddu.

Pte. Joseph Edward Rogers of Fennant Road, Ponciau.

Pte. Allen Lewis, aged 22 of 11 Campbell Street, Ruabon.

Pte. Samuel Philip Corke of Chirk, aged 41. He had served in the Boer War.

Sergeant Arthur Davies died of wounds on 11th May. He was from Chirk.

Pte. James Ellis of Ruabon.

Lance Sergeant Charles Carrington. Born in Bagillt, he worked in the Ruabon Coal Company. He had been a Terrier since 1908.

Pte. George Rowlands of Rhosddu.

L/Cpl William David Evans of Hennessy Terrace, Denbigh. He advanced towards the German trenches but never returned. Pte. D.T.Roberts of Cyffylliog wrote to his cousin Mr. Pendlebury of Denbigh stating that Will had died in hospital.

Albert Edward Myddleton, known as Ted, was the son of Charles and Ellen Myddleton and the brother of Thomas Hugh Myddleton. He died at the base hospital on 11th May. He was buried in Bethune Cemetery. Thomas Hugh Myddleton was serving with the 1st Battalion RWF and was missing in action so it was an awful time for the family. A letter was later written from the War Office to Mrs. Myddleton saying that Thomas was in a Military Hospital with wounds that were not life threatening.

The wounded at Aubers Ridge included the following Denbighites:

Pte. Reginald Lewis, 12 St. Hilary's Terrace suffered a bayonet wound through the arm, rendering it useless. He discharged from the army.

L/Cpr Eleazer Davies, Leicester Terrace was wounded for the second time.. In civilian life he was an Asylum Attendant.

Pte. Edward Williams of Brynfynnon Terrace. Missing, presumed killed. Returned to safety with bullet wound to his mouth.

Pte. Fred Lloyd of the Castle. Wounded and was being treated by the above.

Pte. Edward Lloyd was wounded and hospitalised until July in Manchester.

Pte. Frank Atkinson of the Castle. An asylum attendant. Discharged from the army due to the serious nature of his wounds.

Pte. William E. Pritchard was blasted by a shell, rending one of his arms useless. Dischared from the army in September 1915.

Serg. William David Davies, Hennessey Terrace. Shot and wounded.

Serg. John Caledfryn Davies, Brynffynnon Terrace, wounded.

Pte. Edward Jones, 14 Tower Terrace was wounded.

Pte. Walter Davies, Factory Place, wounded.

Pte. Thomas Myddleton Jones, hospitalised in England.

Pte. D.O. Evans, son of Mr. Meyrick Evans. Hospitalised with frostbite earlier in the war, now wounded. Back in the firing line later in 1915. His brother Luther Evans was in the military.

Pte. Fred Jones 105 Henllan Street, hospitalised in Kent. Back with the battalion later in the year.

Pte. Robert William Ellis, hospitalised in Glasgow.

Some had a lucky escape. Lieutenant Donald Seymour Jones had a shrapnel shell burst a short distance from him as he was going forward on the charge. One of the bullets from the shell went into his clothing, passed through a letter from home and punctured his water bottle where it came to rest.

Warren Lewis:

" *When Reg comes home, as I hope he will, tell him that I was sorry not to see him. But I heard that he had been hit, so I went out to look for him, but could not find him, so I brought some others in. I thought it was my duty to do it, so I did it.*

Sgt. Warren Lewis received the Military Medal for bravery in 1917.

Pioneers

The Battle of Festubert, of which the fight for Aubers Ridge was a part, took place over a number of days and so involved many Battalions of other Regiments.

It is no surprise that there were other Denbigh casualties, both dead and wounded, over the course of this action, mostly from the ranks of the RWF.

Pte. Elias Jones of 79 Henllan Street was reported as missing in action from the 1st Battalion RWF. He was declared killed in action in August. Elias was married to Elizabeth Jones and his name appears on the Le Touret Memorial.

L/Cpl William Owen Hughes, Love Lane, was killed with the 1st Battalion RWF. He has no known grave.

Robert Thomas Jones, known as *Tommy bach* or *Ginge* was a resident of 96 Henllan Street. He was married with two sons, Sam and Bill, and now a daughter, born shortly after his death. She was named France May. Tommy was also with the 1st RWF.

Bodfari born John Parry of 1st RWF was a resident of Park Street, Denbigh, and was killed in action on 16th May.

Pte. Richard Williams was 38 years old and married to Mrs. Margaret Williams. The family home was in Luke Street, St. Asaph. He was killed on 16th May.

Joseph Davies of the Welsh Regiment was killed on 16th May.

On 29th May the Denbigh Terriers found themselves between Verquinnel and La Beuvry, a quiet part of the front line. Some Denbigh men were sent on leave, for some it was their first since Southampton. Lieut. Carless visited friends in Denbigh and Pte. Ellis Williams visited home in Brynffynnon Terrace.

On 4th June Captain Frederick Clough was fit enough to join his men at Cuinchy. This was dangerous territory and notorious for shelling.

On 6th June Pte. David Davies was killed.

On 8th June Pte. Morris Price of Rhosymedre died of wounds.

The Coldstream Guards relieved the Terriers and the Battalion enjoyed some work unloading supplies and ammunition, transporting, and guarding in the town of Bethune. Everyone in the Battalion turned out for the burial of Pte. Morris Price of Rhosymedre who died of wounds on 8th June. Pte. Price was a native of Nefyn.

Captain Peter Foulkes Roberts was now fit enough to join the men.

Officers of 1/4th RWF Mentioned in Sir John French's Despatches were:

Major W.R.Wilson and Captain Thomas Oswell Bury (commanding B Company). Mr. Bury was one of three brothers serving with the Territorials.

Also 2nd Lt. John Arthur Hughes (died of wounds), Acting Sergeant Major R.P.Davies, Lance Sergeant W.Ledsham and Pte. E.Swainson, who had been at Ruthin Grammar School.

Pte. Swainson lived in Rossett prior to the war. In April he was a despatch rider with the battalion and had shown bravery carrying a wounded colleague to safety. He was known as a fine athlete, and had distinguished himself at cricket and hockey.

Sir John French was a personal friend of Mrs. Cornwallis-West of Ruthin Castle. She heard that the Denbighshire Territorials were still without field kitchens and wrote to the General to complain. Field kitchens arrived a week later and a fusilier wrote home to describe the benefits:

" The dinners are now much better, the meat tastes tenderer. The method used to cook it is to use fireless cooking - consisting of boiling all for 20 minutes, then putting it away for two hours in an airtight container to finish it off slowly."

A service was held for the boys killed and wounded in the battle. Leading the singing was Sergt. Major George Wainwright, an accomplished musician, who secured a small harmonium which he played at this service. A few days later he was admitted to hospital with mental and physical exhaustion. He had been in France without a break since November 1914.

Mr. C.W.Lewis had a boot shop on Ruthin Road. His brother Warren Lewis send home all manners of souvenirs which were displayed in the shop window. German, French and Belgian bullets, a piece of a German gun destroyed at Plas Bassee. Rings made out of German shells.

A large draft arrived to bolster the numbers of men in the 4th Battalion. Most came from the Bedfordshire Regiment and the remains of the Yorkshire Light Infantry who had taken a lot of casualties at Festubert.

Many natives of Bedford were recruited as the 2/4th RWF were stationed in Bedford at the time.

On 28th August 7573 Pte. Edward Lloyd was hit by a shell in the trenches and was killed instantly. In civilian life he had been a servant at Plas Captain Farm. He was a native of Nantglyn and had joined the Terriers with his brother Walter Lloyd. Edward was buried near to the trench and like so many others, it was lost as the ground was fought over for the next three years. His name appears on Le Touret Memorial along with thousands of others with 'no known grave'.

Gas held a special fear and the Terriers were attacked by gas shells. Pte. Edward Salibury Jones had to return home with impaired vision and shrapnel wounds after one such attack.

The British also used this weapon. Captain Peter Foulkes Roberts and Captain Howard George Picton Davies (both solicitors in civilian life) led parties of men releasing barrels of the noxious substance against the German lines on the 25th September, the opening day of the Battle of Loos. Both officers became violently sick.

Picton Davies wrote:

"On 19th the gas cylinders were brought up : no vocabulary could express the men's thoughts on those cylinders as they struggled and sweated up the narrow trenches , festooned with detached telephone wires that gripped sometimes the throat , sometimes the feet. By 20th everything was ready. With the approach of Zero Hour on 25th we were ready. At 5.30am the gas was released. On the front of our Division the wind was in the right direction and the right strength. The gas went over well. When the cylinders were exhausted , a smoke screen was put down , the trenches were bridged over with duckboards , and the Infantry , wearing their gas masks , went over at 6.30am."

Pte. Robert Thomas Hughes of Millbank , Llanrhaeadr was killed by a shell on that day, close to Captain Picton Davies who subsequently wrote to the 20 year old's parents. Pte. Hughes had not seen home since November 1914.

Pte. John Williams serving with the 1st Battalion RWF was killed assaulting German trenches. He was 35 years of age and a former Territorial soldier. His mother was Mary Ann Williams , New Road , Castle.

The Loos Offensive claimed two other Denbigh lives:

21 year old Arthur William Winterton Turnour , 2nd Lt. 2nd Rifle Brigade was killed leading his men into action. He was the son of Rev. and Mrs. Turnour , Grove House , Denbigh. There is a plaque commemorating his name in St. David's Church.

John Owen Gilmore of the Scots Guards , a resident of Factory Place , was killed 27th September . He has no known grave and his name is commemorated on the Loos Memorial.

Following Loos , Pioneer Battalions were added to each Division. With the coming of the New Armies and Pals Battalions now being fully trained and ready to fight , the Saturday Soldiers – and the 4th RWF - had had their day as front line infantry. The casualties had been shocking and a new immediate use for these strong men was needed in labouring and trench digging.

A new journey began. They packed up and set off for the south to a quieter sector of the front line. 1916 must surely be a better year someone suggested as they whistled and marched down to the Somme.

"Denbigh National School Roll of Honour , 31st July 1915

4th RWF

Cpl. Alf Boyes , C. Coy , Henllan Street.

Pte.William Clayton , Abrams Lane.

L/Cpl Eleazer Davies , Leicester Terrace.

Pte. Jeremiah Davies.

Pte. Walter Davies, Factory Place.

Sgt. John Caledfryn Davies, Brynffynnon Terrace.

L/Cpl Thomas Albert Davies, Hennessey Terrace.

Sgt. J.H. Emmanuel, Henllan Street.

Pte. Edward Charles Griffiths, Rosemary Lane.

Pte. James Gilmore, Henllan Street.

Pte. T.Herbert Hughes

Pte. William Hughes, 8 Wesley Place.

Pte. Edward Hughes, 8 Wesley Place.

Pte. R.Thomas Hughes, Bryn Goleu, Broomhill Lane.

Pte. Elias Albert Jones, Henllan Street.

Pte. Thomas Jones, 98 Henllan Street.

Pte. David Jones

Pte. Robert Jones, Wesley Place.

Pte. Edward Jones, 14 Tower Terrace.

Pte. W. Pierce Jones

Pte. W.A. Lewis, The Castle.

Pte. Reggie Lewis, 12 St.Hilary's Terrace.

Pte. S. Lincoln Miller

Pte. Robert Parry

Cpl. Thomas Pierce, The Castle.

Pte. W.J.Roberts

Pte.D.M.Roberts

Pte.W.Owen Roberts

Col.Sgt. Thomas Roberts , Henllan Street.

L/Cpl John Roberts

Pte.John Riley , 4 Wesley Place.

Pte. Richard Thomas

Staff Sgt. J.O.Thomas , Park Street.

Pte. Jackie O.Thomas , Park Street.

Pte. T.Morris Williams , Graig Quarry

Pte.J.Lewis Williams , Factory Place.

Pte. Sam Williams

Pte. George Conway Williams

Pte. Edward Williams , Brynffynnon Tererace.

Staff Sgt. Robert Williams , Henllan Street.

Pte. Archie Warren , 8 Ruthin Road.

Pte. Edward James Wright , Beacon's Hill.

Also , killed in action the following:

William Evans , Hennessey Terrace.

Albert Edward Myddleton , Coppy Road.

J.P.Thomas , Park Street."

References:

The Denbighshire Free Press (Microfilm) Denbighshire Record Office , Clwyd Street , Ruthin.

The North Wales Times (Microfilm) Denbighshire Record Office , Clwyd Street , Ruthin.

The Street Names of Denbigh , R.M.Owen , 1981

The Royal Welsh Fusiliers , H.A.Tipping , 1915 , Country Life.

The 4th(Denbighshire) Battalion , Royal Welsh Fusiliers in the Great War , C.Ellis , 1926 , Woodall , Minshall , Thomas and Co. Ltd. , Wrexham.

The Diaries of David S. Foulkes Roberts , Denbighshire Record Office.

The Records of the Royal Welsh Fusiliers Volumes II and III , Dudley Ward , 1926.

The History of the World War 1914-1918 , Liddell Hart , 1934 , Faber & Faber Ltd. London.

1915 : The Death of Innocence, by Lyn McDonald , 1997 , Penguin.

All Rights Reserved. No part of this book may be reproduced in any form or by any electronic or mechanical means – except in the case of quotations – without the written permission from the publisher , Peter Glynn

Printed in Great Britain
by Amazon